Absolute Beginner's
DECOUPAGE

Absolute Beginner's
DECOUPAGE

The Simple Step-by-Step Guide
to Creating Beautiful Decoupage

ALISON JENKINS

WATSON-GUPTILL PUBLICATIONS/NEW YORK

A QUARTO BOOK

Copyright © 1999 Quarto Inc.

First published in 1999 in the United States
by Watson-Guptill Publications,
a division of BPI Communications, Inc.,
1515 Broadway, New York, N.Y. 10036

Library of Congress Catalog Card Number: 98-87522

ISBN 0-8230-0055-9

This book was designed and produced by
Quarto Publishing plc
The Old Brewery
6 Blundell Street
London N7 9BH

Project editor Ulla Weinberg
Art editor/Designer Julie Francis
Photographers Andrew Sydenham, Jon Wyand
Picture researchers Gill Metcalfe, Laurent Boubounelle
Art director Moira Clinch
Assistant art director Penny Cobb
QUAR.ABD

Manufactured in Singapore by Eray Scan Pte Ltd.
Printed in China by Leefung-Asco Printers Ltd.

First printing, 1999

1 2 3 4 5 6 7 8 9 / 07 06 05 04 03 02 01 00 99

CONTENTS

INTRODUCTION

DECOUPAGE IS THE ART AND CRAFT of decorating surfaces with cutout motifs or images. The word itself is derived from the French verb *decouper*, which means "to cut out." The basic principle is simple: choose suitable images, cut them out carefully, glue them on the prepared surface, then seal and finish the project with several coats of varnish.

The art of decoupage has enjoyed a huge revival in recent years, inspired in part by the wealth of printed material available. Papercutting for decorative purposes, however, has existed for many centuries, first in China, where paper was invented about A.D. 105, then in Europe, where paper was introduced during the 12th century. Decoupage as we know it today developed in Italy during the late 17th century and was a popular pastime of the ladies of the court. During the 1800s, following the development of more advanced printing techniques, high-quality prints were produced in great quantities. Such printed material was called "scrap." In Britain, the Victorians eagerly used these images for decorative purposes, and decoupage became a favorite hobby. The production of scraps was a commercial success, and is once again today, in response to the demands of the current decoupage revival.

For those who are new to decorative crafts, decoupage provides an excellent means of creative expression. The only requirements are patience, enthusiasm, and an eye for color. With relatively little effort, it is possible to transform humble household objects into works of art. No surface is too large or small to be given a new lease on life. From a jewelry box to a glass vase to a toy box and even walls and doors, virtually anything can be decorated with decoupage. After overcoming the initial hurdle of getting started in a new craft, the problem may be knowing when to stop, as all decoupage enthusiasts will agree.

Traditional techniques can be used to achieve a modern look.

HOW TO USE THIS BOOK

The aim of *Absolute Beginner's Decoupage* is to introduce the reader to this exciting craft using a foolproof two-stage system for creating elegant decoupage projects.

In each of ten inspiring lessons, Stage One demonstrates a single decoupage technique, then the project in Stage Two shows how this technique can be imaginatively incorporated into a stunning decoupage creation.

This comprehensive volume is rounded out by a gallery of projects to intrigue and inspire the budding decoupage artist.

stage one TECHNIQUE guides you through an essential technique.

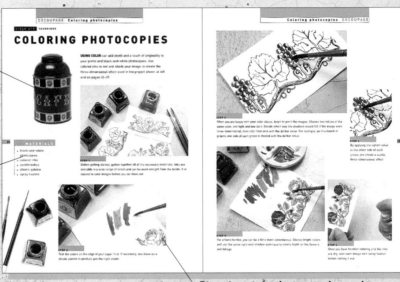

Photograph of project featured in Stage Two.

List of materials needed to practice the technique.

Step-by-step photographs and instructions clearly demonstrate the technique.

stage two PROJECT shows you how to use the technique learned in Stage One to make a delightful project.

Decoupage your project with the templates and motifs provided.

A comprehensive materials list helps you to assemble everything you need.

Step-by-step photographs and instructions show how to use the technique mastered in Stage One in a project.

Helpful tips to ensure success.

Full-page photograph of the finished project.

TOOLS AND EQUIPMENT

AS WITH ANY CRAFT, it is essential to have the right tools for decoupage. Make sure all of the necessary implements are arranged on your work surface before you begin a project.

SCISSORS A small pair of sharp scissors is essential for decoupage. Choose one that feels comfortable in your hand. The blades may be either straight or curved. Keep a larger pair of scissors for cutting away excess paper before doing more intricate cutting. Always keep scissors sharp, and use them only to cut paper.

CRAFT KNIVES Craft knives are perfect for the detailed cutting involved in decoupage work. Keep a stock of replacement blades, since a blunt cutting instrument may damage or tear your paper image. Specialized craft knives with swivel blades are also available; these are ideal for cutting circles and tiny curved edges. Use a larger craft knife, together with a metal ruler, for cutting straight edges and backgrounds.

CUTTING MAT A self-healing cutting mat will protect your work surface when you use craft knives.

BRUSHES It is important to have a variety of paintbrushes, from fine ones for coloring and tinting to large, flat ones for colorwashing and general painting and varnishing.

TWEEZERS Use these for picking up tiny cutouts and for use in three-dimensional decoupage.

RULER AND MEASURING EQUIPMENT A transparent ruler is ideal for measuring and marking, and a metal ruler is essential when cutting straight edges with a craft knife. A compass and protractor measure circles and precise angles.

RAGS AND SPONGES Slightly damp pieces of cloth or sponge are useful for tamping down glued images and for removing excess glue.

ADHESIVES White, water-soluble glue dries clear and is suitable for most decoupage projects. It dries completely in about 20 minutes, so it will allow only slight repositioning while the glue is still wet. Wallpaper paste can be used as an alternative. Silicone glue and double-sided self-adhesive pads produce a raised effect. When gluing, put your images on waxed paper to keep them from sticking to the work surface.

PAINTS Acrylic paints are easy to use and quick-drying, and therefore suitable for most decoupage projects. They are available in a wide spectrum of colors. Latex paints can be used for larger areas and furniture items. Specially formulated paints are available for use on metal, plastics, and ceramics. Some wood or metal surfaces may need to be primed before they can be painted.

INKS Inks come in a variety of colors and are used to color black-and-white prints or photocopies. Thin the ink with water in a plastic mixing palette, and apply it with a brush for a translucent finish.

WATERCOLOR PAINTS AND PENCILS Watercolor paints can be used for colorwashing larger areas of black-and-white prints and copies. Add soft, delicate color to images with watercolor pencils and colored pencils.

PENCILS Use a sharp pencil to mark out decoupage layouts, and a china marker to draw on glass or metal. Carbon paper and tracing paper are used for producing designs and transferring them to decoupage objects.

SPRAY FIXATIVE Seal all your images with a thin coat of fixative. This will keep glue and varnish from seeping through and discoloring the images.

VARNISH When your decoupage is complete, you must apply multiple layers of varnish to protect the cutout images. There are many types of varnish available, but acrylic quick-drying ones are easiest to use. Choose from matte, satin, or gloss finishes. Oil-based polyurethane varnish tends to yellow with time, so use it if an aged effect is required. Available in kits, craquelure varnish produces a crackled, antique appearance.

EQUIPMENT FOR SURFACE PREPARATION Strip off thick coats of old paint and varnish with paint and varnish removers. To remove a light coat, sanding with sandpaper will be sufficient. Also use sandpaper to roughen clean surfaces so that your basecoat can grip. Make sure you have a variety of grades for different types of surface. Wood putty is applied to repair holes, cracks, or irregularities. Use a tack cloth to remove loose, flaking paint and sanding dust.

9

SOURCE MATERIAL

MATERIALS FOR DECOUPAGE projects can be obtained from a wide range of sources. Keep interesting images and scraps of paper or photographs in a box or file until you are ready to use them.

Calendars and color prints are excellent sources for color images.

Copyright-free books on a variety of subjects can provide a treasure trove of images. Just photocopy your chosen image directly from the book and enlarge or reduce to size. Magazines offer a wealth of color images to cut out and use. Colorful wrapping paper is also ideal for decoupage. Reproductions of Victorian "scraps" featuring traditional images are also readily available.

10

In addition to making multiple copies, a photocopier can be used to enlarge, reduce, and reverse images. Color copiers are useful for reproducing real items, such as flowers.

Charts, maps, and sheet music are useful for backgrounds.

Almost any object can be used for decoupage if it has a smooth surface. Wood, papier-mâché, cardboard, metal, plastic, and ceramics are all ideal surfaces. Remember to apply primer if necessary and prepare the surface appropriately (see page 14).

TINTING AND COLORING PRINTS

BLACK-AND-WHITE images are perfect for decoupage as is, but to add a touch of originality to your work, try coloring them yourself.

INKS

Inks impart strong color but remain translucent, so you can see the image clearly through the color. Apply the ink with a paintbrush and let dry.

 12

WATERCOLOR WASH

Watercolor wash, a watery solution of paint and water, gives an image an all-over hint of color. Brush over the print with a large flat brush. Try to avoid creating streaks and blotches of color.

SEPIA TINT

Sepia tint can be added to a background image by rubbing it with a damp tea bag. If the image is large, "stretch" the paper by taping it to a board along each edge with masking tape to prevent wrinkling when the wash dries.

WATERCOLOR PAINTS

Watercolor paints give a pale, subtle effect, which is ideal for coloring in black-and-white images.

SEALING

When you are happy with your colored image, let it dry completely, then seal it by spraying on a thin coat of fixative. The fixative will keep the colors from bleeding when you apply the glue.

COLORED PENCILS

Colored pencils add subtle color to your images. Watercolor pencils, whose colors can be blended with a moistened brush, are also available.

CUTTING

ACCURATE CUTTING is an essential part of successful decoupage. With practice, your skill with scissors and craft knife will improve, and the process will become much easier.

STEP 1
Use large or medium-sized scissors to cut away all unnecessary paper from around your chosen image. Cut close to the print but do not attempt to cut away any fine or intricate areas yet. Keep your work surface clear by throwing away all the excess paper.

STEP 2
Begin to cut accurately around the image with small scissors, holding the paper in one hand and the scissors in the other and slowly feeding the paper into the scissors.

STEP 3
Lay the image flat on a cutting mat and cut out the inside portions and any tricky details with a craft knife. Work carefully, concentrating on one small section at a time.

13

STEP 4
On delicate areas of the image, leave "ladders" (small tags of paper) attaching details to the larger motifs. These can be cut away before gluing.

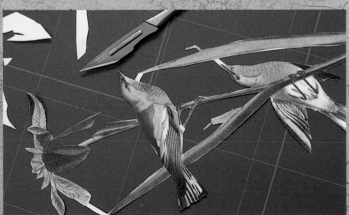

STEP 5
Don't worry if you slip and cut off a small part of your image; just save the piece and position it correctly when you are affixing the image to its background.

SURFACE PREPARATION

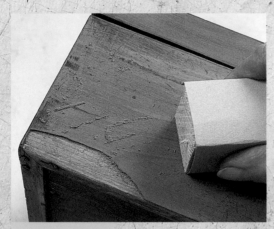

ANY SURFACE—whether it be wood, metal, plastic, papier-mâché, cardboard, glass, or ceramic—can be used for decoupage. No matter what kind of surface you choose, good preparation is the key to success.

STEP 1
Wooden or painted surfaces should be sanded with sandpaper. If there is heavy paintwork or varnish, use a remover to strip them off first. Wipe away dust and paint flakes with a tack cloth. Allow to dry.

14

STEP 2
Using a putty knife, apply wood putty to repair any holes, cracks, or surface irregularities.

STEP 3
When the putty is dry, sand again with sandpaper. Wipe away the dust with a tack cloth and allow to dry.

STEP 4
Apply a coat of white acrylic primer if you are planning to paint the object in a lighter color than the original wood. Allow to dry.

STEP 5
Apply one or two coats of your chosen basecolor. Acrylic and latex paints are suitable for most surfaces, but specially-formulated paint products for metal, glass, and ceramics are also available.

STEP 6
Metal, enamel, or galvanized surfaces should be cleaned with detergent and hot water. Allow to dry completely before applying one or two coats of metal primer.

GLUING AND POSITIONING

ONCE YOU HAVE cut out your images and your project's surface has been prepared, you can begin to glue them in place, using white craft glue or wallpaper paste.

STEP 1
When working on a flat surface, you can easily move your cutouts around until you are satisfied with the design, before fixing each one in place. If you are working on a cylindrical or vertical object, cut a paper template to fit, then lay the template flat on your work surface and plan your design on it.

STEP 2
When you are happy with your design, trace around each of the cutout shapes with a pencil.

STEP 3
Place the template over a piece of carbon paper cut to the same size, then wrap both around your object. Hold them in place with pieces of masking tape.

15

STEP 4
Trace over the original pencil lines to transfer the positions of the cutouts to the object. These markings will be a guide for gluing.

STEP 5
Lay the cutout image, printed side down, on a sheet of waxed paper to keep it from sticking. Using a flat paintbrush or a glue spreader, apply a thin layer of glue or paste. Always work from the center of the image out toward the edges.

STEP 6
If your image is delicate, rub some adhesive directly onto the object with your finger.

STEP 7
Place the image within the traced guidelines. Use a barely dampened sponge to smooth it out, again working from the center to the outside; this removes any air bubbles and ensures even adhesion. Wipe away excess glue, and allow to dry overnight.

BASIC PAINT EFFECTS AND VARNISHING

ALTHOUGH YOU CAN decoupage a surface painted with a single color, most projects will benefit from a more adventurous background. There are a variety of paint effects that can liven up your projects. For all these techniques, you have to do some preparation: prime the surface if necessary, then apply one or two coats of a basecolor; finally, choose a complementary shade to create one of the following paint effects.

SPONGING

Dip a small natural sponge in the second color, removing any excess paint on a paper towel. Using a light, dabbing motion, transfer the paint to the basecoated surface. This creates a mottled effect.

16

COLORWASHING

Use a scrunched-up rag to apply the second color, which has been thinned with water, over the basecoat. This creates a softly colored effect.

DRAGGING

Dip a dry brush into a second color, removing any excess paint on a paper towel. Lightly drag the brush over the dry basecoat to create a subtle, distressed finish.

VARNISHING

After your decoupage design is complete and dry, it is time to apply the first of many coats of varnish. A brush-on formulation should be applied with a good-quality brush that will not shed hairs. Allow the appropriate drying time between coats. The aim is to achieve a perfectly smooth surface. This process may take up to 20 coats and a few days to complete.

OIL-BASED VARNISH

Oil-based polyurethane varnish has a long drying time and a tendency to yellow as it ages. It can be used when an antique appearance is desired.

ACRYLIC VARNISH

This dries very quickly, eliminating the long wait between coats required when oil-based polyurethane varnish is used. The spray version is ideal for small or oddly shaped pieces.

GENERAL TIPS AND HINTS

DECOUPAGE is a simple craft, and you will find that with practice you will gain confidence and your skills will improve. Here are a few helpful hints.

STEP 1

Air bubbles are a decoupage nightmare. Sometimes they appear out of nowhere, spoiling all your hard work. If this occurs, simply slit the bubble with a sharp craft knife to release the air.

17

STEP 2

Use a toothpick or a tiny brush to place a small amount of glue inside. Tamp flat using a damp sponge, then let dry.

STEP 3

Before you begin applying varnish, check that no tiny edges have come unstuck, because these will cause problems later. Use a toothpick or small brush to reapply glue to the edge, then sponge flat.

STEP 4

Before varnishing, make sure that all the glue has been removed from around the images, because any remaining glue may cause discoloration under the varnish. Look out for any telltale shiny spots and gently rub them away using a small piece of dampened sponge. Also, make sure that the surface is free of dust, since any particles will spoil the finish.

STEP 5

Stir the varnish gently before each coat—never shake the can, since this will create air bubbles.

`stage one` **TECHNIQUE**

PREPARING WOOD

IT IS ALWAYS worth spending time at the preparation stage to ensure that the surface of the object to be decorated is in perfect condition. The techniques shown here are useful when embarking on the project shown at left and on pages 20–23.

STEP 1

If your wooden surface has a thick coat of old paint or varnish, you will have to strip it off with a remover. For light coats of paint or varnish, sanding with sandpaper is sufficient. New or unfinished wood should also be prepared with sandpaper to guarantee a smooth surface. To make the job easier, prepare a sanding block: wrap a block of wood in a piece of sandpaper.

HELP!

Take a small piece of old pantyhose and run it over a sanded surface to detect any rough areas you might have missed. Resand with fine-grade paper until the surface is perfectly smooth and flat.

18

MATERIALS

- wooden item
- sandpaper
- block of wood
- paint or varnish remover (optional)
- emery board (if needed)
- wood putty
- putty knife or glue spreader
- tack cloth

STEP 2

Always make sure that you sand with the grain of the wood. Small, intricate areas can be reached using an emery board.

STEP 3

Using a putty knife or glue spreader, fill any cracks or irregularities in the surface with wood putty.

STEP 4

Use the putty knife or glue spreader to scrape off any excess putty. Set the item aside for a few hours while the putty dries and hardens.

STEP 5

When the putty has dried completely, sand with a fine-grade sandpaper until smooth.

STEP 6

Run your fingers over the surface to check for any bumps. At this stage, check for any sharp corners, using sandpaper to round them off slightly.

STEP 7

When you are satisfied that your surface is perfectly smooth, use a tack cloth to wipe away any dust particles. Once it is dry, your box is ready for painting.

BUTTERFLY BOX

GIVE A WELL-WORN jewelry box a new lease on life by combining a simple distressing technique with a swarm of vibrantly colored decoupaged butterflies.

20

MATERIALS

- small wooden box
- wood putty
- putty knife
- sandpaper
- tack cloth
- acrylic or latex paints: blue and cream
- paintbrushes
- butterfly images
- spray fixative
- scissors
- craft knife
- cutting mat
- white craft glue
- waxed paper
- sponge
- acrylic brush-on varnish, satin finish

STEP 1

To prepare the surface of the box for painting, fill any cracks or irregularities with wood putty. Sand until the surface is perfectly smooth, then wipe with a tack cloth to remove dust particles. When the surface is dry, apply one or two coats of blue paint, allowing the first coat to dry before applying the second.

STEP 2

Once the basecoat has dried, load a clean, dry brush with a scant amount of cream paint. To create a faded, distressed look, skim the hairs of the brush over the surface so that the paint is applied in light streaks.

STEP 3

Choose large butterfly images to decorate the lid and sides of the box. Seal each image with spray fixative and allow to dry before cutting it out.

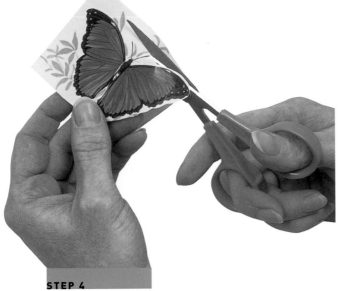

STEP 4

Cut carefully around each butterfly image, using small, sharp scissors to remove excess paper.

STEP 5

Lay the cutouts on a cutting mat and use a craft knife to cut around small or intricate parts, such as the antennae.

STEP 6

Once you have cut out several images, you can begin to arrange a pleasing design on the box. It may take a few attempts to achieve the right look.

STEP 7

Cut out a small square of waxed paper and lay it flat on your work surface. Using a flat paintbrush or small glue spreader, apply a thin coat of white craft glue to the back of each cutout, being careful not to tear the spindly parts.

STEP 8

Position the butterfly cutouts on the lid of the box. While the glue is wet, you can make slight adjustments to the layout.

STEP 9

When you are happy with the positioning, smooth each butterfly down with a piece of damp sponge, making sure that all the edges adhere firmly and that there are no trapped air bubbles.

22

STEP 10

Repeat steps 6–9 to glue butterflies to each side of the box, smoothing each one with a damp sponge as before. Allow to dry.

STEP 11

Apply three or four coats of satin-finish acrylic brush-on varnish, allowing each coat to dry before applying the next.

To make a matching set for a dressing table, decorate a lamp base or cotton ball holder with the same butterfly motifs.

stage one TECHNIQUE

COLORING PHOTOCOPIES

USING COLOR can add depth and a touch of originality to your prints and black-and-white photocopies. Use colored inks to tint and shade your image to create the three-dimensional effect used in the project shown at left and on pages 26–29.

STEP 1

Before getting started, gather together all of the necessary materials. Inks are available in a wide range of colors and can be used straight from the bottle. It is easiest to color images before you cut them out.

24

MATERIALS

- black-and-white photocopies
- colored inks
- paintbrushes
- plastic palette
- spray fixative

STEP 2

Test the colors on the edge of your paper first. If necessary, mix them on a plastic palette to produce just the right shade.

STEP 3

When you are happy with your color choice, begin to paint the images. Choose two values of the same color, one light and one dark. Decide which way the shadows would fall if the image were three-dimensional, then color that area with the darker value. For example, on this bunch of grapes, one side of each grape is shaded with the darker value.

STEP 4

By applying the lighter value to the other side of each grape, you create a subtle, three-dimensional effect.

25

STEP 5

For a floral border, you can be a little more adventurous. Choose bright colors and use the same light-and-shadow technique to create depth on the flowers and foliage.

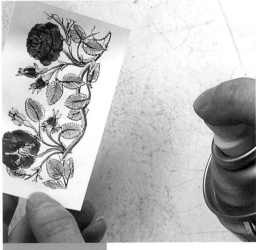

STEP 6

Once you have finished coloring and the inks are dry, seal each image with spray fixative before cutting it out.

`stage two` PROJECT

COFFEE CANISTER

BRIGHTEN UP a dark corner of your kitchen with a delightful French-style coffee canister. Decoupage two more in matching colors—one for tea, one for sugar—to make a complete set.

MATERIALS

- tin canister
- metal sandpaper and sanding pad
- rag and sponge
- metal primer
- paintbrushes
- acrylic paint: pale purple
- lettering and floral border
- colored inks: yellow, blue, red
- spray fixative
- scissors and craft knife
- cutting mat
- metal ruler
- china marker
- waxed paper
- white craft glue
- glue spreader (optional)
- lint-free rag
- acrylic brush-on varnish, matte finish

STEP 1

To remove old paint and varnish, sand the surface of the metal canister, using a sanding pad and sandpaper suitable for metal. Wipe the canister with a damp rag to remove any dust particles, then allow to dry.

STEP 2

To prepare the surface for painting, apply a coat of metal primer with a paintbrush and allow to dry.

STEP 3

Apply a basecoat of acrylic paint. You may have to apply two coats to cover the primer fully.

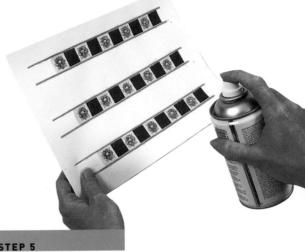

STEP 4

While the basecoat is drying, paint the letters and border using colored inks and a paintbrush. Use shading to create a three-dimensional effect (see page 25).

STEP 5

When the ink is dry, seal the letters and border with spray fixative before cutting.

STEP 6

Roughly cut away the excess paper from around each letter with small scissors.

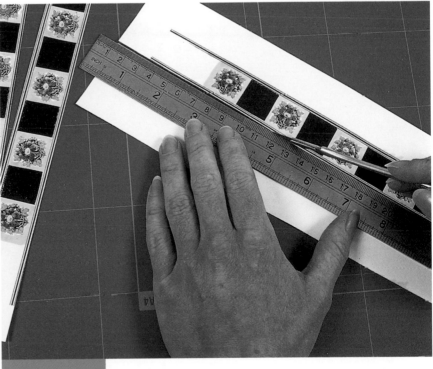

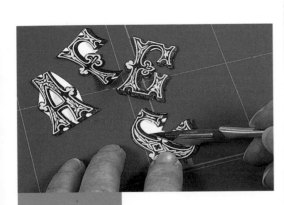

STEP 7

Place the letters on a cutting mat, then carefully cut around the edges of each one with a craft knife.

STEP 8

For the floral border, cut along the straight edges using a craft knife and a metal ruler. You may need to prepare more than one border to make it fit around the canister.

Why not make a matching
set of herb and spice tins
to sit in a row on your
kitchen shelves?

STEP 9

When the basecoat is dry, use a china marker
to indicate the position of the lettering.

STEP 10

Lay the borders facedown on a
sheet of waxed paper, and
apply a coat of white craft
glue to the back of each one
using a flat paintbrush or glue
spreader. Position the floral
border on the canister and
smooth with a damp sponge.

STEP 11

Glue the letters into position on the canister in
the same way as the floral border.

HELP!

After coloring a photocopy,
allow it to dry completely
and seal with spray fixative.
This ensures that the colors
will not run or smudge
when smoothing or
varnishing.

STEP 12

When the glue is completely dry, wipe away the
china marker guidelines with a damp, lint-free
rag. Apply three coats of matte-finish acrylic
varnish, allowing each coat to dry before
applying the next.

28

ANTIQUING

OIL-BASED POLYURETHANE varnish tends to yellow as it ages, which is exactly the effect required when creating an antique appearance. You can take the antiquing process a little further by adding burnt umber oil paint to the varnish. This effect is used in the project shown at left and on pages 32–35.

30

MATERIALS

- wooden object, painted and decoupaged
- artists' oil paint: burnt umber
- rags
- mineral spirits
- small glass jar
- oil-based polyurethane varnish
- paintbrush

STEP 1

When all glue and paint on the wooden object is dry, you can begin the antiquing process. Practice on the base of the object until you are confident. First pick up a small amount of oil paint on a soft cloth and rub it over the surface, concentrating it in the corners and along the edges of the decoupage image.

STEP 2

Rub off most of the excess oil paint with a clean rag. There should be just a hint of darkness left on the surface and around the decoupage image.

STEP 3

In a small jar, mix a little oil paint with just enough mineral spirits to make the paint fluid.

STEP 4

Blend the mixture with a small amount of oil-based polyurethane varnish. Mix well with a brush. You can add more oil paint if the effect is too subtle.

STEP 5

Apply a thin coat of the tinted varnish with even strokes, avoiding runs and streaks.

STEP 6

As you apply subsequent coats of varnish you will see that the color will begin to darken. Allow each coat of varnish to dry before applying the next.

stage two PROJECT

ELEGANT WASTEBASKET

ELEGANT CLASSICISM is the theme for this simple wastebasket, proving that even the most ordinary objects can be stylish.

STEP 1

Use an electric drill to make a hole through the base of the wastebasket at each corner. To make the feet, attach four small, rounded, wooden drawer knobs from the inside with long wood screws.

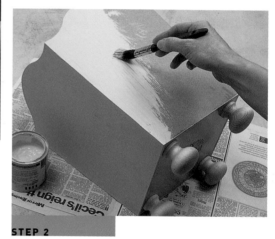

STEP 2

Apply two coats of light yellow latex paint both inside and outside the wastebasket, allowing the first coat to dry before applying the second.

32

MATERIALS

- wooden wastebasket
- electric drill
- four wooden drawer knobs plus screws to fit
- latex paint: light yellow
- paintbrushes
- classical sculptural image plus ornamental corner
- spray fixative
- scissors and craft knife
- cutting mat
- metal ruler
- masking tape
- pencil
- waxed paper
- white craft glue
- glue spreader (optional)
- sponge and soft rags
- artists' oil paint: burnt umber
- mineral spirits
- oil-based polyurethane varnish, satin finish

STEP 3

Select a classical image and corner, then photocopy them, enlarging or reducing them as necessary. Seal each image with spray fixative before cutting it out. Cut around each one roughly with sharp scissors to remove the excess paper.

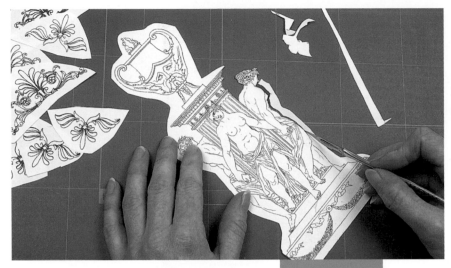

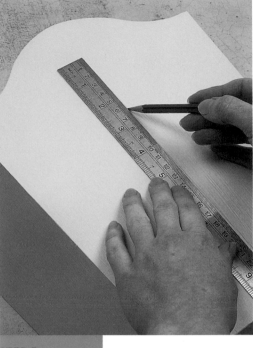

STEP 4

Place the roughly cut pieces on a cutting mat. Cut accurately around each image using a craft knife.

STEP 5

Using a ruler, measure and mark the center of each side with a faint pencil line as a guide to positioning the central motif.

STEP 6

Lay the wastebasket on its side and arrange the central motif and decorative corner pieces. If necessary, hold the pieces in place temporarily with small tabs of masking tape.

STEP 7

Using a faint pencil line or small dots, mark the position of each piece. Repeat this on all four sides of the wastebasket.

STEP 8

Lay the cutout images facedown on a piece of waxed paper and, using a brush or glue spreader, apply a thin layer of white craft glue to the back of each one.

STEP 9

Carefully position the cutouts on the wastebasket, using the pencil marks as guides. Smooth out the glued images with a damp sponge to eliminate any air bubbles that may be trapped.

HELP!

Resist the temptation to apply the varnish thickly to complete the project quickly, as this may result in runs and streaks. Always apply varnish in thin, even coats, and allow each coat to dry before applying the next.

STEP 11

When the glue is dry, rub a little undiluted oil paint along the corners and lightly over the surface of the wastebasket with a soft rag. Use another rag to remove excess oil paint to leave just a hint of darkness around the image and over the basecoat. Leave the oil paint to dry.

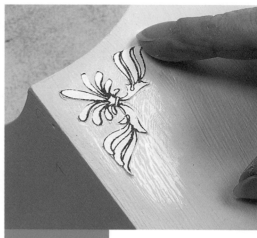

STEP 10

For the small corner pieces, it is easier to use your finger to apply the glue to the wastebasket itself, rather than to the back of the cut piece. Place the corner pieces into position and wipe away any excess glue with a damp sponge.

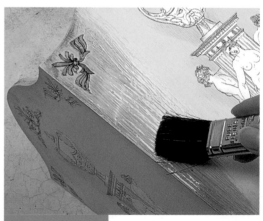

STEP 12

Mix the oil-based polyurethane varnish with oil paint and mineral spirits (see page 31). Apply four coats of tinted varnish, allowing each coat to dry before applying the next.

For a different look, try decoupage with enlargements of old family photos or old black-and-white prints .

stage one **TECHNIQUE**

MAKING BORDERS

PHOTOCOPIERS CAN BE USED not only to produce multiple copies of your chosen image, but also to make reduced, enlarged, and mirror images. Use repeat images in different sizes to create an unusual border for the project shown at left and on pages 38–41.

STEP 1

Some photocopiers will produce mirror images. If you do not have access to such a machine, you can copy your image on a piece of acetate. When you turn the acetate over and make another copy, you will produce a mirror-image effect.

36

MATERIALS

- photocopies
- acetate (optional)
- scissors
- metal ruler
- pencil
- plain sheet of paper
- white craft glue
- cutting mat
- craft knife

STEP 2

Reduce the image, using a photocopier, by an increased percentage each time. These images can be joined together to make a graduated border. Cut closely around each of them with scissors.

STEP 3

Using a metal ruler and pencil, draw a baseline for the border strip on a plain sheet of paper.

STEP 4

Glue the images on the baseline so that the animals (here, elephants) are following each other in an orderly fashion, trunk to tail. Photocopy the new border and make a mirror-image copy. Put the borders onto a cutting mat and cut them into strips with a craft knife.

STEP 5

Use a pencil and ruler to draw an angle of 45 degrees at one end of each strip so that the animals will appear to meet face-to-face at the corners.

37

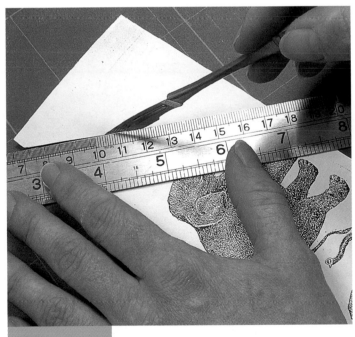

STEP 6

Put the strips on the cutting mat, and use the craft knife and ruler to cut along the pencil lines. These angled ends will fit together to form neat, mitered corners.

STEP 7

Place the mitered strips together to check the fit. If the angles are not correct or the images are not ideally placed, recut and try again. Use the final strip as a template for cutting the subsequent border pieces to complete your project. You will need to join several together to make complete borders.

stage two **PROJECT**

ANIMAL TOY BOX

ANY CHILD would be thrilled to fill this cheerful toy box with treasures. In addition to being a colorful addition to any room, the box can be used to practice counting and to identify colors and animals.

38

MATERIALS

- wooden toy box
- white primer
- paintbrushes
- electric drill with ½-in (2-cm) spade bit
- sandpaper
- metal ruler
- pencil
- masking tape
- latex paints: red, blue, yellow, green
- animal images
- watercolor paint: red, blue, yellow, green
- plastic mixing palette
- spray fixative
- scissors
- craft knife
- white craft glue
- sponge
- acrylic brush-on varnish, satin finish
- short length of colored rope for handles

STEP 1

Apply a coat of white primer to the toy box with a paintbrush and allow to dry.

STEP 2

Drill two holes at each end of the toy box with the electric drill to hold the rope handles. Rub off any rough edges with sandpaper.

STEP 3

Use the pencil and metal ruler to mark out the positions of the border strips around the edge of the lid and around each side, then divide the space between the borders into a grid of equal squares. The number of squares depends on the size and shape of your box.

STEP 4

Outline one of the squares with strips of masking tape. Paint the square with one color of latex paint, let it dry, then remove the masking tape.

STEP 5

Repeat to paint the remaining squares, each in a different color, first on the same side, then on the other three.

STEP 6

Photocopy animal images, reducing or enlarging each one to fit inside the squares, and make some mirror images. Add a watercolor wash to each to complement the painted squares. Allow to dry, then seal with spray fixative before cutting out.

HELP!

Make sure that the border strips adhere well to the box, particularly on the corners and other areas that will receive a lot of wear and tear.

STEP 7

Cut roughly around each animal image with small scissors, then use a craft knife to cut accurately around the outline.

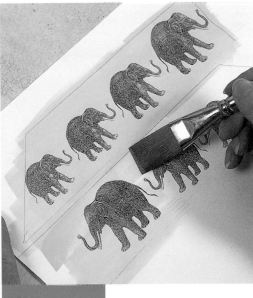

STEP 8

Make elephant trail border strips (see pages 36–37) and apply a watercolor wash to each.

39

STEP 9

When the watercolor wash is dry, color each elephant in a complementary color. Let dry, then seal with spray fixative.

STEP 10

Using the craft knife and metal ruler, cut and miter the elephant trail border to fit the border marked on the box.

40

STEP 11

Apply white craft glue to the back of each animal cutout with a flat paintbrush or glue spreader. Position one cutout in each colored square. Smooth the images down with a damp sponge to eliminate any air bubbles and to ensure that all the edges adhere firmly to the surface of the box.

STEP 12

Apply glue to the back of each border piece, position them on the box, and smooth down with the damp sponge. Allow to dry overnight.

STEP 13

Apply four coats of satin-finish acrylic varnish, allowing each coat to dry before applying the next. Make sure that the varnish is nontoxic and safe for use on children's furniture and toys. Finally, thread rope handles through the holes at each end of the box and tie the ends in a knot on the inside.

For a different look, use large numbers or letters and have fun with counting or spelling games.

stage one TECHNIQUE

CURVED SURFACES

MAKING A FLAT paper image follow the curvature of the object to be decorated is easily achieved with the aid of a sharp craft knife and a few strategically placed cuts. Practicing this technique will help you to achieve the look of the project shown at left and on pages 44–47.

42

MATERIALS

- large wine glass
- cutout decoupage image
- craft knife
- cutting mat
- white craft glue
- paintbrush or glue spreader
- sponge

STEP 1

The convex surface of the glass will cause the decoupage cutouts to wrinkle. To counteract this, make slits with a craft knife where the wrinkles form. The cutout image can then be flattened. Try this with a dry cutout first. Press the image on the inside of the bowl to see where the wrinkle or crease appears.

STEP 2

Lay the cutout image on a cutting mat and make slits from the back using a craft knife.

STEP 3

Place the slit image in the glass. The slits will overlap when pressed against the glass so the cutout lies flat.

STEP 4

Apply white craft glue to the front of the cutout image. The amount of glue is important here: too much and it will ooze out; not enough and the image will not adhere.

STEP 5

Place the glued image inside the glass and press into position with your fingers.

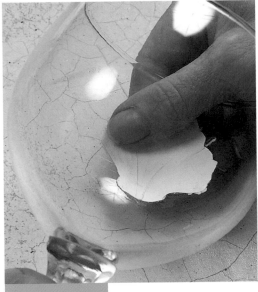

STEP 6

Smooth the back of the glued image with your finger to remove any air bubbles—these will be easy to see from the right side of the glass.

43

STEP 7

Wipe away any excess glue from the inside with a damp sponge. Be very careful not to disturb the position of the cutout.

STEP 8

When the glue is completely dry, it will be colorless and clear.

`stage two` **PROJECT**

FAN GLASS VASE

CURVED GLASS is perfectly smooth, and therefore an ideal surface for decoupage. This plain glass vase has been transformed into a beautiful object. Display it on its own or insert a fresh plant in its pot for a special effect.

STEP 1

Seal the fan images with spray fixative and allow to dry before cutting them out carefully with small scissors.

MATERIALS

- colored fan images
- spray fixative
- small scissors
- large glass bowl
- removable adhesive mounting pads
- china marker
- pencil
- cutting mat
- craft knife
- waxed paper
- white craft glue
- flat paintbrush or glue spreader
- sponge
- lint-free rag
- masking tape
- metallic spray paint: silver
- acrylic spray varnish

STEP 2

Beginning at the bottom and working up, position the fans temporarily around the vase on the inside, using tiny pieces of removable adhesive mounting pads. As you work you will see where to make the slits so the images will lie flat (see page 42).

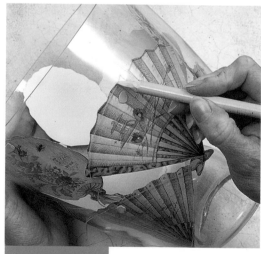

STEP 3

When you are satisfied with the design, trace the position of each piece on the outside of the glass with a china marker. As an extra precaution, you can number the cutouts on the back with pencil.

44

STEP 4

Remove the cutouts and place them facedown on the cutting mat. Make small slits where necessary, cutting from the center of the piece toward its lower edge.

STEP 5

Place each cutout on a piece of waxed paper, and apply a thin coat of white craft glue to the front, using a flat paintbrush or glue spreader.

STEP 6

Position the fan cutouts inside the vase, overlapping row by row from the base toward the rim. Use the china marker lines as guides.

HELP!

Follow the design or pattern lines as closely as possible by making small slits in the paper prints. These cuts will become almost invisible when the pieces are overlapped.

STEP 7

Smooth out the glued images periodically using a damp sponge to wipe away excess glue and to expel any air bubbles.

Decoupage under glass was a popular trend in the 19th century, and was recently rediscovered.

STEP 8

When all the larger images are in position, fill in any gaps with smaller cutouts.

STEP 9

Using a damp, lint-free rag, wipe the china marker guidelines from the outside of the glass.

STEP 10

When the glue is dry, stick a strip of masking tape around the outside top edge of the vase and apply a coat of metallic spray paint to the inside. Allow to dry completely and remove the tape.

STEP 11

Apply four coats of clear spray varnish to seal the inside of the vase. Note that the vase should not be immersed in water, but may be wiped clean with a damp rag. If you want to use it for fresh flowers, place a smaller glass vase filled with water inside.

stage one TECHNIQUE

INTRICATE CUTTING

YOUR SKILLS with a craft knife and scissors will improve as you practice, and intricate cutting will not seem such a daunting task. There are no shortcuts at this stage, and it is worth taking your time to practice for the project shown at left and on pages 50–53.

48

MATERIALS

- image
- spray fixative
- small scissors
- pencil
- craft knife
- cutting mat

STEP 1

Select an image that has lots of intricate parts and will allow you to practice your cutting skills. Seal the image with spray fixative and allow to dry before cutting; this will strengthen the paper, making it more resistant to tears.

STEP 2

Roughly cut around the outside using small scissors to remove excess paper.

STEP 3

Using a pencil, draw "ladders" to connect spindly parts of the image to the central section. Building in ladders will help minimize tearing and damage while you are cutting out the other sections.

STEP 4

With a craft knife, begin to cut out and remove the inside spaces, leaving the ladders attached.

STEP 5

Cut accurately around the outside edges of the image as well.

49

STEP 6

When the image is cut out completely and you are ready to glue, you can cut away the ladders. You are now ready to position your cutouts.

`stage two` **PROJECT**

LETTER SORTER

DECORATE A HUMDRUM letter sorter with a delicate tangle of beautifully colored birds and foliage. Because the images have many thin parts, it is easy to mingle them to achieve an intricate design.

50

MATERIALS

- letter sorter
- latex paint: red
- paintbrushes
- images of birds and foliage
- spray fixative
- small scissors
- cutting mat
- craft knife
- masking tape
- pencil
- waxed paper
- white craft glue
- glue spreader (optional)
- sponge
- toothpick
- acrylic brush-on varnish, matte finish

STEP 1

Apply two basecoats of latex paint to the letter sorter and allow to dry. A removable central divider makes painting and decoupage easier.

STEP 2

Choose the bird images carefully, and seal each one with spray fixative before starting to cut out.

STEP 3

While the paint dries, begin to cut out the delicate birds and foliage. Cut away the excess paper from around the images first with small scissors.

STEP 4

Lay the images on a cutting mat, and cut out the smaller areas with a craft knife. Remember to include "ladders" to attach delicate parts to larger areas, and leave them in place until you are ready to glue (see page 49).

STEP 5

When the paint is dry, you can arrange the cutouts in a pleasing and balanced design, using tiny tabs of masking tape to hold each image in place.

51

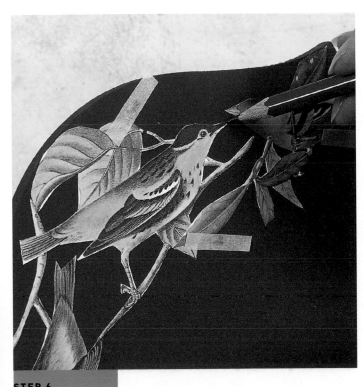

STEP 6

Indicate the position of each image with small pencil marks.

STEP 7

When you are satisfied with your design, remove the cutouts one by one and then carefully snip away the "ladders."

STEP 8

Lay the cutouts facedown on a piece of waxed paper and apply a thin coat of white craft glue to the back of each with a small paintbrush or glue spreader. Work gently to avoid tearing any tiny parts.

For a more contemporary look, use old postage stamps from around the world for a combination of collage and decoupage.

STEP 9

Position each cutout on the letter sorter. You can make small adjustments to the layout while the glue is still wet.

STEP 10

When you are happy with the layout, sponge away any excess glue, and allow the piece to dry completely.

52

STEP 11

When dry, check that all the small, intricate parts are adhering firmly to the surface. If not, apply a little additional glue with a toothpick, sponge clean again, and allow to dry.

HELP!

Always use a sharp blade and have plenty of replacement blades handy— a dull blade can tear and damage your images.

STEP 12

Apply three coats of matte-finish acrylic varnish, allowing each coat to dry before applying the next.

stage one TECHNIQUE

USING TEMPLATES

YOU CAN EASILY use templates to cut your own patterns and decorative motifs from colored paper. Just take a basic motif and customize it to suit your project. Practice this technique before embarking on the tray project shown at left and on pages 56–59.

54

MATERIALS

- border template
- pencil
- tracing paper
- plain white paper
- cutting mat
- craft knife
- small scissors

STEP 1
Photocopy a border template, then trace just half the length of the pattern using a pencil and tracing paper.

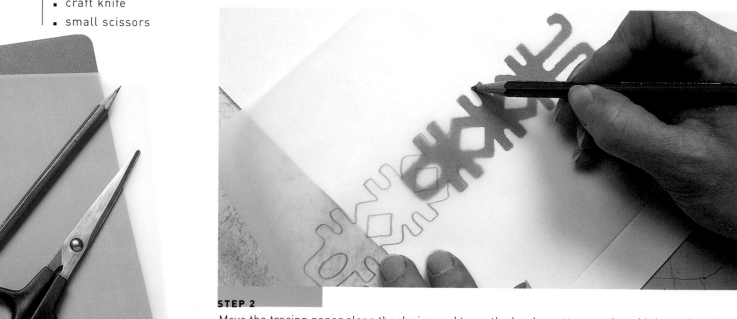

STEP 2
Move the tracing paper along the design and trace the border pattern again; add the end section when the tracing measures half the length of the object you are planning to decorate.

STEP 3

This technique helps you to create borders to fit any length.

STEP 4

Fold a piece of paper in half and use the template to trace the border on it, placing the rounded end on the fold.

STEP 5

Place the folded paper on a cutting mat and carefully remove the central parts with a craft knife.

STEP 7

Unfold the paper to reveal a perfect mirror-image border strip. It is much more efficient to cut the border in this way than to trace and cut the complete border.

STEP 6

Cut around the outside edges with scissors.

MEXICAN TRAY

VIVID COLORS and bold stylized images and patterns are used to decorate a plain tray in a Mexican style. It is ideal for serving drinks outside on hot summer evenings.

56

MATERIALS

- wooden tray
- acrylic or latex paints: light green, red
- paintbrushes
- Mexican-style images: animal, zigzag border, border
- tracing paper and pencil
- plain and colored paper: red, yellow, blue
- craft knife
- small scissors
- spray fixative
- white craft glue
- glue spreader (optional)
- sponge
- acrylic brush-on varnish, satin finish

STEP 1

Apply two coats of green latex paint to the inside and outside of the tray, allowing the first coat to dry before applying the second.

HELP!

If you have difficulty gluing the square border to the tray, simply cut it into sections and apply it one piece at a time.

STEP 2

Use a small paintbrush to paint the edges of the tray and the insides of the handle red. Allow the tray to dry completely while you cut out the decoupage motifs.

STEP 3

Photocopy the border, zigzag border and animal motif, enlarging them to fit the sides and base of your tray. Trace the motifs from the enlarged copies with tracing paper and a pencil, and transfer them on paper to produce templates.

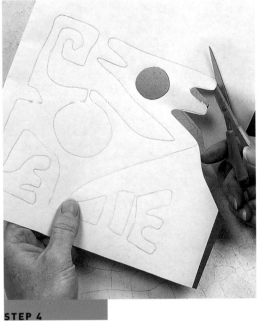

STEP 4

57

Fold a piece of blue paper in half. Place the animal template on the folded paper, and cut out the image: First remove the inner parts with a craft knife, then cut around it with small scissors. Unfold the blue paper to reveal two mirror images.

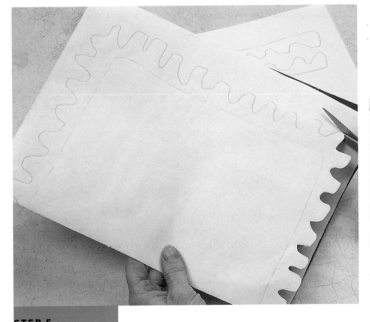

STEP 5

Place the zigzag border pattern on folded red and yellow paper, and cut out each border with small scissors.

STEP 6

If necessary, extend the other border design to fit the sides of the tray (see page 55). Cut out carefully from yellow and blue folded paper with a craft knife and scissors.

Bold motifs such as these also work well in striking black and white.

STEP 7

Seal all the cutout pieces with spray fixative, and allow to dry before gluing and positioning on the tray.

58

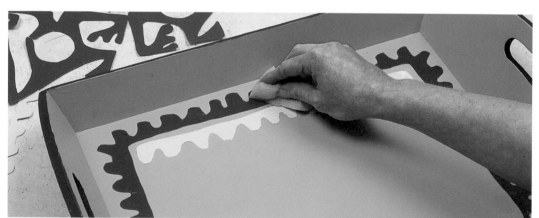

STEP 9

Apply three coats of acrylic varnish to the front and back of the tray, allowing each coat to dry completely before applying the next.

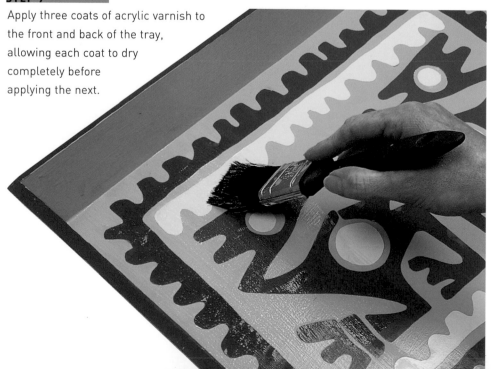

STEP 8

Apply a thin coat of white craft glue to the back of the cutouts, using a brush or glue spreader, then begin positioning. Start with the border pieces, smoothing each one out with a damp sponge to make sure that the edges adhere firmly to the surface. Finally, position the two animal motifs in the center. Allow the glue to dry before wiping away any glue residue from around the motifs with a damp sponge.

CRAQUELURE

CRAQUELURE IS an amazing effect achieved by using a kit containing two varnishes that dry at different rates. Within a short time, thousands of tiny cracks will appear. Accentuated with artists' oil paint, as in the project shown at left and on pages 62–65, it gives the appearance of aged varnish.

60

MATERIALS

- painted and decoupaged surface
- craquelure varnish kit
- paintbrush
- hair dryer
- artists' oil paints: burnt umber, metallic gold
- rags

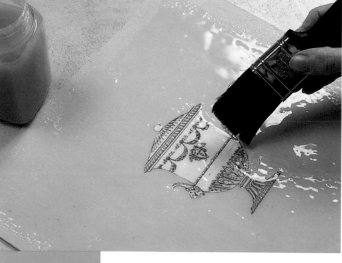

STEP 1

Apply the first coat of craquelure varnish to the painted and decoupaged surface. Set aside for about 20 minutes until it feels dry to the touch.

STEP 2

Apply the second coat of craquelure varnish, brushing smoothly, and allow to dry.

STEP 3

You can speed up the drying process at this stage by using a hair dryer set on medium.

STEP 4

As the second coat of varnish dries, you will see tiny cracks appearing over the surface.

STEP 5

Pick up some oil paint on a soft rag and rub it over the surface. Make sure that the pigment is worked into all the tiny cracks. Here, burnt umber oil paint complements the ochre background.

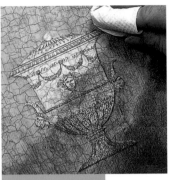

STEP 6

Wipe off all the excess oil paint from the surface with a clean rag.

STEP 7

This picture shows the finished effect.

STEP 8

You can also use contrasting colors to enhance the craquelure varnish effect. Here metallic gold is laid over a blue background.

STEP 9

Use a clean rag to wipe away all the excess oil paint as before.

STEP 10

The finished result is more subtle than using burnt umber. This technique works best over a dark basecoat.

61

STEP 9

When the glue is dry, wipe away any excess glue from the paintwork with a damp sponge.

STEP 10

Using a flat paintbrush, apply stage 1 of the craquelure varnish kit. This will appear white when wet, but will dry clear in 15–20 minutes.

STEP 11

When the first coat of varnish is dry, apply stage 2 of the craquelure kit, which is a colorless coat. Leave the second coat to dry. If you want to speed up the process, you can use a hair dryer. As the second coat dries, tiny cracks will appear all over the surface.

STEP 12

When the surface of the box is cracked and dry, take a small amount of burnt umber oil paint on a soft rag and rub it into the cracks.

The effect produced by craquelure varnish is also ideal for ceramic items, giving them a really authentic cracked glaze appearance.

STEP 13

Wipe away all the excess oil paint with a clean rag. When you are satisfied with the result, leave the box overnight for the oil paint to set. Apply a coat of acrylic brush-on varnish to seal.

3-D DECOUPAGE

YOU CAN CUT and mount two-dimensional images so that they appear realistic and three-dimensional. Practice with a simple image, and build up layers to achieve an effect that is used in the project shown at left and on pages 68–71.

MATERIALS

- several copies of the same image, cut out and sealed with spray fixative
- waxed paper
- white craft glue
- paintbrush or glue spreader
- spare painted practice board
- sponge
- small scissors
- double-sided adhesive pads
- silicone glue
- tweezers

STEP 2

Place the cutout on a background board that is painted a complementary color. Smooth flat using a damp sponge.

STEP 1

Select an image that is suitable for a three-dimensional effect. Place one of the sealed cutouts facedown on waxed paper and apply a thin coat of white craft glue on the back.

STEP 3

Decide which parts of the image should appear in the foreground, closest to you, and which parts should recede into the background.

STEP 4

Take a second copy of the image and begin by cutting away the parts that should appear to be farthest away.

STEP 5

Place double-sided adhesive pads on the back of the cutout. These work well for attaching the larger pieces. Peel off the backing papers.

STEP 6

Place the cutout in position on the background piece. You will see how the three-dimensional effect begins to form.

STEP 7

Cut out smaller or "closer" pieces of the image. Experiment with different sections to see which work best. To attach small cutout pieces, squeeze a few drops of silicone glue to the back. The glue will remain thick even when dry.

STEP 8

Use tweezers to pick up small pieces. This way, you can position them more accurately without getting glue on your fingers.

STEP 9

By layering sections of the decoupage image, you create a striking, three-dimensional effect.

Fruit and floral images work very well for three-dimensional projects, but there is a wealth of other images you can use.

STEP 8

Using small scissors, cut away a little more of the background for the third layer, and fix into position with adhesive pads as before.

STEP 9

Continue to build up the layers, each time cutting away a little more of the image.

STEP 10

Small leaves and foliage can be given a little extra shape by drawing them over the blade of a pair of scissors to make them curl.

STEP 11

As you reach the foreground of the image, the pieces will become smaller, and it will be necessary to use silicone glue and tweezers to fix the pieces into position. Apply a few drops of glue to the back of the cutout piece.

STEP 12

Place the glued image into position. Using tweezers ensures accuracy and keeps your fingers clean.

STEP 13

For the frame, miter four pieces of wooden batten with a saw to fit the edge of the backing panel. Use wood glue to fix the joints. When dry, attach the frame to the backing panel with brads. Paint it green, then drag it with red paint.

70

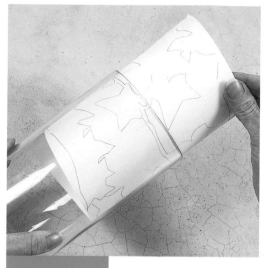

To achieve a similar effect, use other natural forms, such as large leaves with pretty shapes and colors, or pressed flowers.

STEP 9

Slip the template back inside the lamp, holding it in place, if necessary, with small tabs of masking tape.

STEP 10

Place each cutout vine facedown on a piece of waxed paper, and apply a coat of white craft glue to the back using a flat paintbrush or glue spreader.

STEP 11

Following the pencil guidelines, place each vine into position on the glass, and smooth down with a damp sponge. Wipe away excess glue as you work.

STEP 12

When the glue is dry, apply two or three coats of acrylic spray varnish, allowing each coat to dry before applying the next.

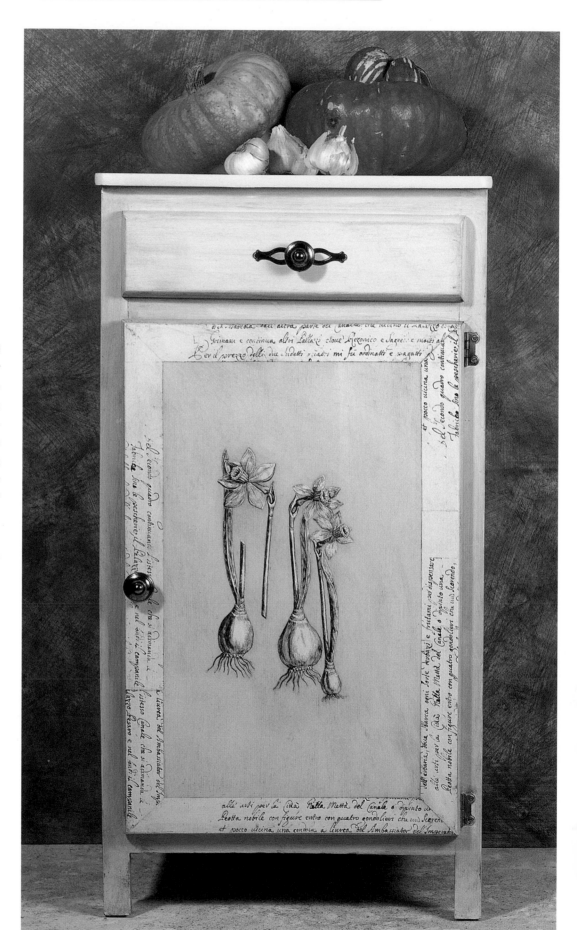

KITCHEN CUPBOARD
Linda Barker

Used for kitchen storage before the days of built-in cabinets, this old-fashioned cupboard has been rescued from a junk shop and given a new lease on life with a coat of cream paint and traditional black-and-white images and text. As a finishing touch, the cupboard has been given a distressed appearance with brown furniture wax.

TOY BOX
Angela Shaw

Scenes of a childhood from long ago are recreated by the tin drums, soldiers, rocking horses, and steam trains on this traditional children's toy box. The bright colors of the decoupage images are set off by the subtle yellow background.

STRAWBERRY TRAY
Maggie Pryce

Succulent, ripe fruit adds a sumptuous touch to a simple wooden tray. Strawberries, whether used enlarged or actual size, are a perfect motif for decorating trays used for delicious afternoon coffee and tea sessions.

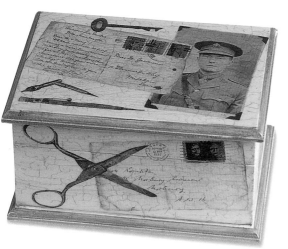

LETTER BOX
Maggie Pryce

This small box was decorated with tinted photographs, drawings, and copies of old letters to give it an old-fashioned look.

WHITE BOX WITH FLOWER WREATH
Angela Shaw

A circlet of full-blown roses and delicately colored flowers are charming embellishments for this romantic hope chest, a perfect place for a new bride to keep treasured letters, cards, and keepsakes as reminders of her wedding day.

FISH FIRE SCREEN
Sandra Hurst Chico

Bold, witty, and adventurous, this fishy fire screen uses simple cutout shapes on a pale blue background. Tissue paper has been used to achieve a translucent underwater effect.

SHELL VASE
Linda Barker

The intricate and inspiring shapes of shells are used to great effect on this silvered glass vase, ideal for a contemporary home. The images have been glued to the inside of the vase, then sealed with many coats of varnish to prevent water from seeping through.

SHELL FRAME
Graham Day
Tiny repeated images make an intriguing decoration for a wide, modern picture frame. The natural color of the background has been tinted around the edges with a delicate wash of lilac.

SEA CREATURE CUPBOARD
Linda Barker
Black-and-white photocopies of shells and sea creatures are matched by rows of swirling text to give this simple cupboard a maritime look. A coat of tinted acrylic glaze was added and then stippled to achieve a mottled effect.

FISH SHELF
Tamara von Schenk
A set of shelves, unusual yet traditional in style, has been painted in a modern combination of blues and aqua, and each shelf has been decoupaged with realistic images of fish in different sizes.

EVERYDAY OBJECTS

No object is safe from the eager hands of the enthusiastic decoupage artist. Even the most commonplace objects can be given star treatment by decorating them with paint and cutouts. With careful preparation and finishing, the objects are no less useful for being beautiful and decorative.

KITCHEN CUPBOARD
Linda Barker

The witty use of utensils and cutlery makes this cupboard feel quite at home in a kitchen. This idea could be adapted, using different themes to suit other rooms in the house. The final varnish finish has been scratched with sandpaper and then rubbed with a colored wax polish. The color is deposited in the scratches on the surface for a simple distressed look.

MONEY WASTEBASKET
Deborah Schneebelli-Morrell

A reminder of the perils of throwing your money away, this wastebasket will bring a smile to the home office. Collect low-denomination notes or receipts and mementos from a vacation or business trip abroad for use in small decoupage projects. Simply glue in place, then apply a matte varnish finish.

SHEET MUSIC BOX
Graham Day

Sheet music has an elegance all its own, and is here used to great effect, giving a hint of what might be stored in the box. The sheets have first been tinted with tea to achieve an aged sepia look.

89

POSTCARD FRAME
Graham Day

The backs of postcards are the unexpected decorative material for this simple, rectangular picture frame, providing intriguing half-visible messages from faraway destinations. The stamps add an interesting touch to the monochromatic color scheme.

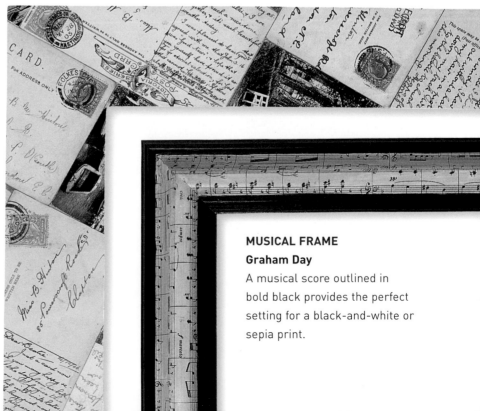

MUSICAL FRAME
Graham Day

A musical score outlined in bold black provides the perfect setting for a black-and-white or sepia print.

CONTEMPORARY

Although decoupage is considered a traditional craft, this by no means restricts its decorative usage. Contemporary images can be used to create a modern, up-to-the-minute look. Some of the pieces shown here and on the following pages display an inspired and adventurous use of materials, color, and imagery. Be brave, and don't be restrained by convention.

90

CLOCK
Gabriel Semphill
Zodiac motifs set into fine, lacy motifs and multipointed stars are the basis of this finely worked decoupage clock. The clock's simple shape and pale cream background with a delicate craquelure finish subtly suggest antiquity.

VASE
Juliette Pierce
This vase, which is constructed from papier-mâché over an armature of chicken wire, is a highly original piece. The stylized decoupage images are further enhanced by the bold use of color and the decorative painted borders.

CHOCOLATE BOX
Deborah Schneebelli-Morrell

Vibrant metallic chocolate wrappers have been used here to cover a small cardboard box, showing how easy it is to improvise and use your imagination. A small golden tassel has been added to the lid to complete the project.

CLOCKS
Juliette Pierce

Clock-watching takes on new meaning with these inventive, indulgent timepieces. They were individually handcrafted by the artist, and decorated in a bold and exuberant fashion. The techniques employed remain simple, proving that great things can be done using basic knowledge and a vivid imagination.

BANANA TABLE
Tamara von Schenk

A jaunty yellow-and-white check background is given an amusing Caribbean flavor with a border of banana bunches. Again, a traditional-looking piece of furniture has been transformed into a delightful contemporary work of art.

CHAIR
Juliette Pierce
More a throne than a chair, this work of art proclaims the skills of a talented and inspired decoupage artist, and takes us willingly into the realms of fantasy.

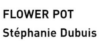

FLOWER POT
Stéphanie Dubuis
Terracotta, with its porous texture and warm color, makes the perfect base for this decorative pot. It was created by applying copies of botanical illustrations, then lightly sponging the pot with a terracotta shade of paint.

INDEX

94

CREDITS

Quarto would like to thank the following for supplying pictures or objects for the gallery section:

Stéphanie Dubuis, Paris, France (Botanical Tray and Flower Pot first created for MARIE CLAIRE IDÉES, June 1998)

Howson Vaughan Découpage Furniture & Accessories, Shrewton, Wiltshire, England

Juliette Pierce, Hove, Sussex, England

Maggie Pryce Decoupage and Gilded Gifts, Warminster, Wiltshire, England

Angela Shaw, Guildford, Surrey, England

Tamara von Schenk, London, England

All other photographs are the property of Quarto Publishing plc.

The author would also like to thank the following for supplying material and equipment for the projects featured in this book:

Homecrafts Direct, PO Box 38, Leicester, England (materials and equipment for specialist crafts)

Mamelok Press Ltd, Northern Way, Bury St. Edmunds, Suffolk, England (decoupage "scraps")

The Painted Finish, Hatton, Warwick, England (blanks, paint and varnish, decoupage sheets)

Scumble Goosie, Stroud, Gloucestershire, England (blanks, decoupage sheets, paint, glazes and varnish)

Index prepared by Diana Le Core.